A Robbie Reader

Class Trip

WASHINGTON, D.C.

Claire O'Neal

PUBLISHERS

P.O. Box 196
Hockessin, Delaware 19707
Visit us on the web: www.mitchelllane.com
Comments? email us: mitchelllane@mitchelllane.com

Mitchell Lane

PUBLISHERS

Boston • New York• Philadelphia
San Antonio • San Diego
Washington, D.C.

Copyright © 2010 by Mitchell Lane Publishers

All rights reserved. No part of this book may be reproduced without written permission from the publisher. Printed and bound in the United States of America.

PUBLISHER'S NOTE: The facts on which the story in this book is based have been thoroughly researched. Documentation of such research can be found on page 45. While every possible effort has been made to ensure accuracy, the publisher will not assume liability for damages caused by inaccuracies in the data, and makes no warranty on the accuracy of the information contained herein.

Printing   1   2   3   4   5   6   7   8   9

Library of Congress Cataloging-in-Publication Data

O'Neal, Claire.
  Class trip Washington, D.C. / by Claire O'Neal.
    p. cm. — (Robbie reader, class trip)
  Includes bibliographical references and index.
  ISBN 978-1-58415-809-7 (library bound)
  1. Washington, (D.C.)—Juvenile literature. 2. School field trips—Washington, D.C.—Juvenile literature. I. Title.
  F194.3.O54 2010
  975.3—dc22
                                    2009001109

PLB

CONTENTS

The U.S. Capitol Building in Washington, D.C. The Supreme Court has met there since 1801; the House of Representatives since 1807; and the Senate since 1810. Right: The Washington Nationals' mascot, Screech

The Field Trip Secret

Natalie sat at her desk, thinking about summer break. She glanced out the classroom window at the beautiful June day outside. Would her family go on vacation this year? Her parents usually took her on a special trip every summer, but they hadn't said anything yet. Natalie was a little suspicious, especially because all her friends in class had said the same thing—their parents were being unusually quiet, too. It was almost as if some big secret was being kept from the fourth-graders.

Mr. Porter entered the room just as the bell rang, holding a stack of papers. All the kids looked up at the front desk. "Good morning, class," he said.

"Good morning, Mr. Porter," they echoed.

Mr. Porter was finishing the school year with a geography unit on United States cities. For the last month, Natalie had learned about many of the biggest cities in the country, like New York City, Boston, and Philadelphia. Together, the class read books, searched the Internet, watched movies, and gave reports to

The United States President lives in the White House, at 1600 Pennsylvania Avenue NW in Washington, D.C. The first president to move in was John Adams in 1800.

learn as much as they could. They had listened to Mr. Porter telling them all about his travels and the famous things he'd seen—museums, parks, plays. When Mr. Porter told his famous travel stories, Natalie felt as if she were walking down an old, busy street, one full of the history of the many people who had walked there before. She wished she could visit the places in her geography lessons instead of just hearing about them.

"This week we'll continue our unit on U.S. cities by learning about what is perhaps the most important city in the country. It's our nation's capital, Washington, D.C.," Mr. Porter announced. Natalie knew Washington, D.C., wasn't far from Newark, Delaware, where she lived and went to school, but she'd never been there. Her parents had told her she would enjoy it more when she was older.

Mr. Porter continued, "Each of you will be responsible for researching different aspects of Washington, D.C., either through books in our school library or on the Internet. At the end of the week, we'll use our research to make a guidebook for kids just like you who might visit the city."

He smiled, then said, "We'll be using those books ourselves when we visit Washington, D.C., on a weeklong field trip this summer." He held part of his stack of papers out to the class. When Natalie recognized the permission slips, she gasped in surprise along with everyone else.

Mr. Porter had to wait a long time for the class to settle down. "Your parents are already in on the surprise," he said. "I let them know ahead of time because I needed their help. Did you know you have to write a letter to your **Congressperson** to get permission to visit the White House?" He waved another stack of papers with seals on them. "These are letters from one of our Congressmen, Representative Mike Castle, granting admission to each of you. Our government doesn't just have important

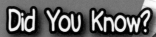

Did You Know?

The vice president and family live in the Admiral's House, a small estate at 34th Street and Massachusetts Avenue, on the grounds of the United States Naval Observatory. In 1977, Walter Mondale, vice president to Jimmy Carter, became the first vice president to live there.

Washington, D.C.

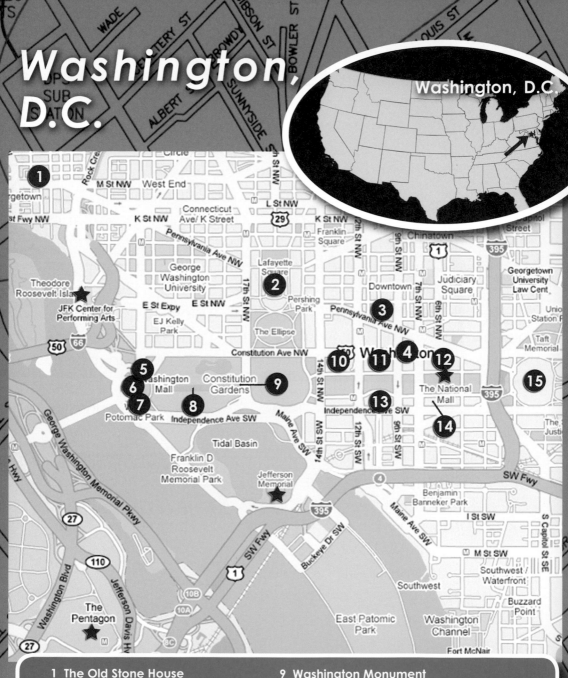

Washington, D.C.

1 The Old Stone House	9 Washington Monument
2 White House	10 National Museum of American History
3 J. Edgar Hoover FBI Building	11 National Museum of Natural History
4 National Archives	12 National Gallery of Art
5 Vietnam Veterans Memorial	13 Smithsonian Castle
6 Lincoln Memorial	14 National Air and Space Museum
7 Korean Veterans Memorial	15 Capitol Building
8 Reflecting Pool	

The Marine Corps War Memorial, found just outside Arlington National Cemetery, honors all U.S. Marines who died serving the country. The statue re-creates a famous photo of World War II marines raising the American flag on the Japanese island of Iwo Jima.

people and important laws, but also important secrets. Security is very tight, especially around Independence Day, when we will visit."

Natalie was thrilled! How awesome it would be to watch fireworks in Washington!

Mr. Porter continued, "You can't really enjoy a visit to D.C. without learning a little American history beforehand. With a week, we'll have time to see lots of the many museums and monuments there. The sights are so much more meaningful, however, when you know the stories behind them. We will spend all this week preparing for our trip by learning as much as we can about this great, historic city. We have a lot to do, so let's get started!"

Gilbert Stuart's painting of George Washington. Dolley Madison saved the painting from the British in 1814. Right: Washington and L'Enfant picking the placement of the city

Washington's Plan Fulfilled

On July 9, 1790, Congress passed the Residence Act. This law created a special **federal** district to be the government's permanent home. Congress named the new capital Columbia after the explorer Christopher Columbus. However, Congress left it up to the President to decide exactly where the District of Columbia should be. President George Washington knew the perfect spot—a mosquito-ridden swamp near Mount Vernon, his plantation in Virginia.

George Washington knew the young country would be a great one. He hired an **ambitious** city planner from France, Pierre L'Enfant, to transform the backwoods location into a world-class capital. L'Enfant designed an organized grid of streets with wide avenues and plentiful parks and green spaces. At the center of it all would be a new house for Congress, the Capitol Building, and, of course, a home for George Washington.

Surveyor Andrew Ellicott mapped out the boundaries of a perfect, 10-square-mile diamond of land along

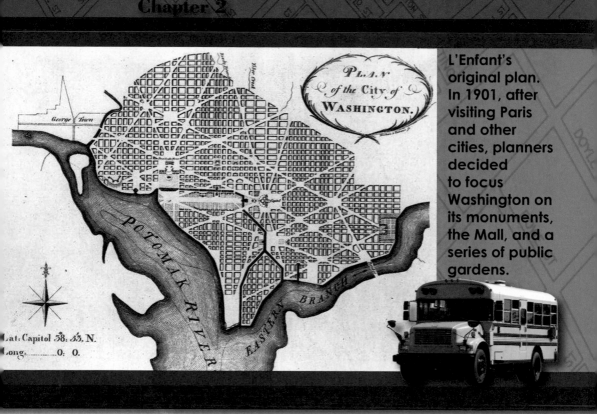

L'Enfant's original plan. In 1901, after visiting Paris and other cities, planners decided to focus Washington on its monuments, the Mall, and a series of public gardens.

the Virginia-Maryland border. One of Ellicott's assistants was Benjamin Banneker, a free black man who was a brilliant mathematician and inventor. Construction began on the president's house on October 13, 1792—the 300th anniversary of Columbus's arrival in the New World. On September 18, 1793, George Washington laid the first stone of the Capitol Building, where Congress would meet. In 1800, the government began moving in, even though neither building was completely finished. John Adams, the second president, became the first to live and work in the President's House.

The new government buildings did not stand for long. On August 24, 1814, during the War of 1812, the British invaded the new capital city and burned nearly every government building to the ground—including the President's House. A popular story says that Dolley Madison, then the First Lady, ran back into the burning mansion to rescue a painting of George Washington. Foul weather forced the British to abandon its attack on D.C. The President's House and the Capitol were rebuilt, but many original buildings were lost forever. Legend has it that the restored President's House was nicknamed The White House when it was repainted white.

British Burn the Capitol, 1814, **by Allyn Cox, is in Cox Hall of the Capitol Building. In the painting, the Capitol is ablaze in the background while British soldiers continue to destroy the rest of the city.**

BRITISH BURN THE CAPITOL · 1814

The Old Stone House in Georgetown is the oldest building in Washington, D.C. Built by a cabinet maker in 1765, it was originally used as a house and a shop.

There were serious talks about moving the capital city instead of rebuilding it. In the beginning, George Washington's city was empty instead of grand. Oliver Wolcott, the secretary of the treasury under John Adams, wrote: "There are few houses in any one place, and most of them small, miserable huts, which present an awful contrast to the public buildings." Officials dreaded living there. They disliked the hot summers, cold winters, and lack of things to do. In 1842, famous British author Charles Dickens visited Washington and was disappointed by the "spacious avenues that begin in nothing and lead nowhere." In 1846, Virginia took back the land it had donated to the city. Since then, the Potomac River has formed D.C.'s southwest border. Virginians feared the loss of their slaves in the area because a young Congressman from Illinois promised to **abolish** slavery.

That man, Abraham Lincoln, would become president in 1861 and revolutionize the town in more ways than one. Almost as soon as Lincoln assumed office, the Civil War began. Union troops rushed into the empty District of Columbia and used it as their headquarters. Many bloody battles were fought close by because the Confederate capital of Richmond, Virginia, was less than 100 miles away. The National Mall, an open park between the Capitol Building and the White House, became a camp for Union soldiers. It also served as an outdoor hospital for the wounded. Among those who helped the soldiers was army nurse Clara Barton. Her experiences inspired her to create the American Red Cross.

When Abraham Lincoln delivered his Emancipation Proclamation speech in 1862, the city's population exploded again. Over 40,000 free blacks and escaped slaves came to live in the district. They were encouraged by Lincoln's promise for a better life. Their arrival set the stage for D.C. to become an important center of learning, culture, and society for African-Americans.

Lincoln Reading Emancipation Proclamation

The early twentieth century brought even more people to the city. After the Great Depression, President Franklin D. Roosevelt established the Works Progress Administration. It provided jobs in the construction business, making new government buildings. World War II also opened more jobs in the government. The new workers took interest in their city. Many monuments and parks were built to make D.C. more beautiful. D.C.'s population reached its highest ever—802,178 people—in 1950.

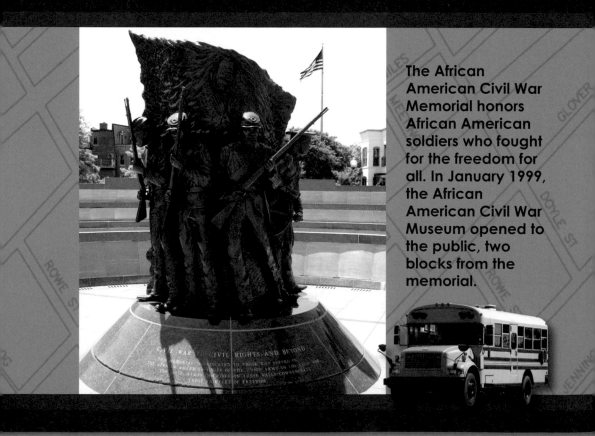

The African American Civil War Memorial honors African American soldiers who fought for the freedom for all. In January 1999, the African American Civil War Museum opened to the public, two blocks from the memorial.

Though the Pentagon is one of the world's largest office buildings, with over 17 miles of hallways, it is designed so that staff can walk between any two points inside in less than seven minutes.

The late twentieth century brought new leadership to the town. Walter Washington, an African American, was elected the first mayor of the district in 1975. Only African Americans have been elected to that position since. D.C. continues to enjoy a population that is racially and culturally diverse, fitting for the capital city of a "melting pot" nation.

On September 11, 2001, **terrorists** crashed a passenger jet into the Pentagon, the headquarters of the Department of Defense located near Washington, D.C. Almost 200 people were killed. Since then, security in the nation's capital has been tight, especially at national treasures and tourist **attractions** like the Washington Monument and the White House.

WASHINGTON, D.C.

Kids sailing on the Potomac, a river rich in history. Right: Pocohontas with son

From Backwoods to Bullets

The people and culture of Washington, D.C., have changed greatly over time. **Anthropologists** believe that the Algonquin people settled the hilly, marshy area of Washington, D.C., more than 4,000 years ago. These native peoples lived across much of northeastern North America. The Algonquins who lived along the Potomac and Anacostia Rivers called themselves the Powhatan tribe. Men of the tribe hunted deer and bear and fished for trout in the Potomac River. Women stayed in the village and grew crops such as corn, squash, and beans.

British explorers arrived at Jamestown, Virginia, in 1607 to make the first permanent English city in the New World. John Rolfe, a settler of the Jamestown colony, introduced Virginia farmers to sweet tobacco from Bermuda. Rolfe became rich and important by farming and selling tobacco to England. The success of tobacco brought more British colonists. They made permanent homes in Georgetown and Alexandria, Virginia, towns that still exist today.

Unfortunately, the colonists and the Powhatans fought bitterly from the start, killing each other and destroying crops. The only peace between the groups came during the eight years after the Powhatan chief's daughter, Pocahontas, married English colonist John Rolfe in 1614. But when Pocahontas's father died in 1622, the new chief wanted revenge on the colonists. He led the Jamestown **Massacre** on March 22, 1622, in which almost 350 colonists were killed. Despite the danger, new colonists kept arriving from England. After many deaths on both sides, by 1648 there were so few Powhatans left that they agreed to a permanent peace with the colonists. The natives had all but disappeared by 1690.

The Jamestown colonists built a fort to protect their settlement from the natives, but they would have starved without the help of the native Powhatans.

The U.S. president addresses the entire Congress in the Capitol. The office of each congressperson employs dozens of people—but these are just a small fraction of the government jobs available in D.C.

The Potomac and Anacostia Rivers were important to the natives and original settlers. Today, they provide the south boundary of D.C. However, the rest of the city looks very different from what the natives and colonists knew. Thanks to L'Enfant, D.C. is a grid of streets, interrupted by circles and spokes, that connect important federal buildings with major roads and parks. The Capitol Building marks the district's center. D.C.'s "Main Street" is Pennsylvania Avenue, a spoke that connects the Capitol to the White House.

The city is designed around the government in more ways than one. Its economy depends on the federal government. The government provides nearly 25 percent of all D.C. workers with jobs. Other jobs come from education, research, health care, and banking. However, compared to other U.S. cities and states, steady and reliable government jobs give Washington, D.C., a very low **unemployment** rate combined with high average pay.

Even so, the town is split painfully between the haves and the have-nots, and has been for decades. In the first half of the 1900s, photographers took many pictures of alley houses, where the very poor lived right across the street from well-kept government buildings. Even after the year 2000, D.C. was suffering from high crime and inferior schools. After many gun murders in 1995, the owner of the National Basketball Association's Washington team decided to change the team's name from the Bullets to the Wizards. By 2009, nearly 20 percent of all D.C. residents were living in poverty.

The haves, such as wealthy businessmen and politicians, usually choose to live out of town. Indeed, the only president native to the Washington, D.C., area was George Washington. His family estate, Mount Vernon, still stands 16 miles south of the city and is a popular tourist attraction. Even he lived in the suburbs!

Washington's carriage at Mount Vernon

Though D.C. is home to the federal government, the city is run by a mayor and the Council of the District of Columbia. The Council is made up of 13 representatives from different **wards**, or neighbor-hoods, of the city. The mayor and council members are elected every four years. The council decides on the town budget and laws.

However, because so much federal business happens in the district, Congress has the right to change the local laws. Also, though D.C. residents pay federal taxes, the district is not a U.S. state and does not have a seat in Congress. Many residents are unhappy that Congress interferes with their town's business, without giving them a say in Congress. In 2000, some were so fed up that they successfully campaigned for new D.C. license plates that say "Taxation Without Representation." The slogan was made famous by American colonists during the Revolutionary War as a reason to fight against British rule.

Did You Know?

The District of Columbia is not a state, but is treated like one in some respects. Compared to the U.S. states, Washington, D.C., is the most crowded. It has the least amount of land, but more people per unit area than any other state.

Washington, D.C. **DC VOTE** TAXATION WITHOUT REPRESENTATION

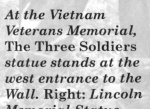

At the Vietnam Veterans Memorial, The Three Soldiers statue stands at the west entrance to the Wall. Right: Lincoln Memorial Statue

4

Made to Be Seen

Washington, D.C., was made to be seen. It is one of the most popular American tourist destinations. It has history, arts, sports, culture, parks, museums, and monuments. Best of all, since many attractions are supported by taxpayer dollars, admission is free.

Most tourists like to start at the National Mall. The Mall is a large, open park between the Capitol and the Lincoln Memorial, and it features many important monuments and museums. Near its center is the Washington Monument, built to honor the nation's first president. At just over 555 feet, it is the world's tallest stone structure. A shallow, rectangular pool of water called the Reflecting Pool lies between the Washington Monument and the Lincoln Memorial. The National Mall has been the site of many **protests** against the government, marches for important causes, and memorable speeches. On August 28, 1963, Martin Luther King Jr. delivered his famous "I Have a Dream" speech from the steps of the Lincoln Memorial.

Chapter 4

The Smithsonian Castle, built in 1855, is the oldest building on the National Mall. It houses the Smithsonian Information Center and the central offices for the institution.

The Mall is home to many departments in the government, such as the Department of Justice, the Department of Agriculture, and the Internal Revenue Service. More interesting to the Mall's visitors, however, may be the Smithsonian Institution, the world's largest complex of museums. In his will in 1826, British scientist James Smithson **bequeathed** about $500,000 to the United States. The money was to be used "for the increase and **diffusion** of knowledge among men." Today more than 30 million people visit each year to see the 136 million objects in its collections. The nineteen Smithsonian museums—which include the National Air and Space Museum, the National Museum of Natural History, the National Museum of American History, and the National Zoological Park (a few miles away)—are all free to the public.

If you prefer sports to museums, you can follow one of D.C.'s many professional teams. In the winter, hockey fans cheer for the Washington Capitals, home of star left wing Alexander Ovechkin. The Capitals share an arena (the Verizon Center) and team colors with the district's basketball **franchise**, the Washington Wizards. The Wizards are the brother team to Washington's WNBA team, the Mystics. In 2005, local baseball lovers cheered as the Montreal Expos relocated to Washington, becoming the Washington Nationals. And don't forget five-time NFL champs the Washington Redskins, who play in nearby Landover, Maryland. Tennis pro Pete Sampras was born in D.C.—he ranked as the world's number one male tennis player for six years in a row, with seven Wimbledon championships, five U.S. Open titles,

Clinton Portis, Redskins

and two Australian Open titles to his name. If you like soccer, join the enthusiastic fans in Robert F. Kennedy Memorial Stadium to watch the D.C. United, one of the most successful American soccer clubs.

D.C. also loves the arts. The world-famous John F. Kennedy Center for the Performing Arts

In Black: Luciano Emilio, D.C. United

27

Late March brings the National Cherry Blossom Festival, when sweet-smelling pink blossoms appear on the thousands of cherry trees in the district. The festival celebrates Japanese culture in honor of the gift of the cherry trees from the people of Tokyo in 1912.

provides a stage for the National Symphony Orchestra, the Washington National Opera, and the Washington Ballet. Additionally, five performers each year receive the widely admired Kennedy Center Honors. D.C.– area theater is respected as well. The Shakespeare Theatre Company is considered one of the world's best. And the district has a great tradition in jazz music. D.C. native Duke Ellington easily ranks among the most famous

Did You Know?

A hidden D.C. treasure is Rock Creek Park. At over 2,000 acres—twice as large as Central Park in New York City—Rock Creek provides a quiet home for wildlife right in the middle of town.

American musicians ever, and was a huge celebrity during the early twentieth century. Ellington composed over 3,000 songs during his fifty-year career and has been honored with 13 Grammys, a Pulitzer Prize, and a Presidential Medal of Freedom.

A trip to D.C. involves a lot of walking, so visitors should know what to expect when it comes to the weather. The climate of Washington changes each season. Spring brings some rain and pleasant temperatures (60–70°F). The town is famous for its hot, humid, and generally uncomfortable summers. Temperatures can reach 90°F in July and August. Fall temperatures, like spring, are mild and pleasant. Winters can be cold and even snowy, as temperatures dip to 20°F between December and February. Tourists will enjoy D.C. the most during the spring and fall.

A 14-foot-tall African bull elephant has greeted visitors to the National Museum of Natural History since 1959. Right: Tyrannosaurus rex fossil

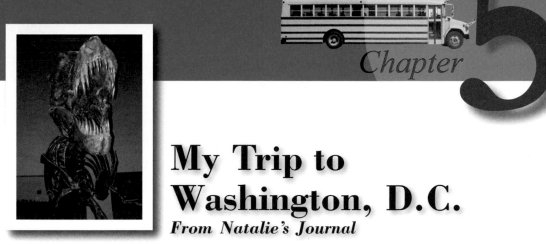

My Trip to Washington, D.C.

From Natalie's Journal

Now I get to experience this city I've been learning about! My first impression? For such a big city, Washington, D.C., feels wide and open. Maybe it is because of the wide streets and all the parks. We also didn't feel trapped in a car or bus. The places we visited were close enough to each other that, once we got downtown, we walked everywhere.

It helps, too, that no building in D.C. can be taller than the dome of the Capitol Building. Did you know the dome is made out of iron, and weighs almost 9 million pounds? We learned that on our tour of the Capitol. The building has two wings: the north for the Senate and the south for the House of Representatives. They join at the Rotunda, whose roof makes the dome. While we were there, Congress was on a break in honor of Independence Day week, but our guide led us to the visitor galleries upstairs anyway. She said people could watch Congress at work in the chambers, and even meet Congress members in person at their offices in nearby buildings.

At the National Archives Building, we saw the actual document that created Congress—an original copy of the U.S. Constitution. The National Archives Building keeps public records of all kinds. It was no surprise, then, that we also saw an original Declaration of Independence and the Bill of Rights there.

The next stop was the National Museum of American History. There we saw the original American flag that inspired Francis Scott Key to write "The Star-Spangled Banner" in 1814. We also saw Dorothy's ruby slippers from the movie *The Wizard of Oz*. My favorite exhibit was "The American Presidency: A Glorious Burden." We learned about what it must be like to be president, including living with your family in the White House. My friend Matthew and I took turns standing on a presidential **podium** and delivering speeches about how it was time for lunch.

Next, we visited the White House. Our guide said we weren't allowed in the President's living quarters, but we did see many beautiful rooms filled with antique furniture and famous paintings. We found out that the White House even has its own bowling alley!

We spent our week visiting more of D.C.'s many museums. We saw priceless paintings at the National

Did You Know?

The National Museum of Natural History and the National Air and Space Museum are two of the most visited museums in the world.

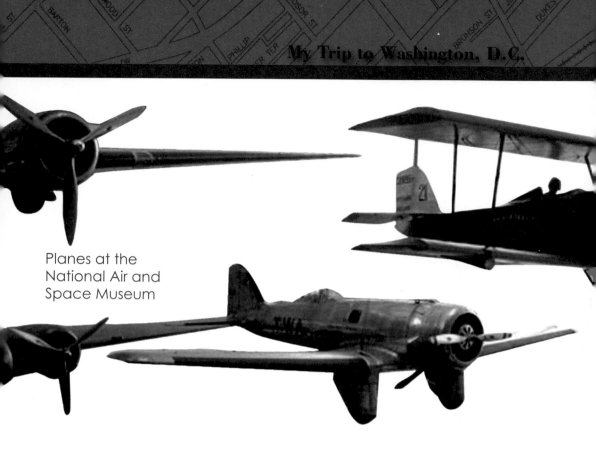

Planes at the
National Air and
Space Museum

Gallery of Art. They have the only Leonardo da Vinci painting in the Western Hemisphere! At the Bureau of Engraving and Printing, we watched sheets of uncut dollar bills roll off the presses. Matthew's favorite was the National Air and Space Museum, where missiles, airplanes, and even spaceships hung from the ceiling. Anybody who loves dinosaurs would enjoy the halls full of skeletons at the National Museum of Natural History. It also had an insect zoo and the famous Hope Diamond. In my opinion, the coolest buildings we saw were the Federal Bureau of Investigation and the International Spy Museum. The Spy Museum has gadgets and technology that real spies used. At the FBI, we saw confiscated weapons and investigators doing real crime-scene investigation. We even

A 1930s spy recording device used records!

watched a real agent practice shooting at a firing range!

Mr. Porter jokingly called July 3 our Memorial Day, since we saw so many statues. Many of the most famous monuments and memorials are close together, clustered around the Washington Monument. We started with the Vietnam Veterans Memorial. Over 58,000 names of soldiers killed or missing from the war are carved into two black stone walls sunk into the ground. I helped Matthew find his grandpa's name. Other kids touched the names of strangers, looking at the flowers and teddy bears left behind by friends and relatives. To remember the soldiers who fought in the Korean War, a group of large statues represents soldiers walking together in action. Mr. Porter told us the long black wall at that memorial was specially **sandblasted** to show wartime scenes. One plaque told us that 54,246 U.S. soldiers died in the Korean War. After seeing the memorials, I think all of us agreed with another plaque nearby that said "Freedom Is Not Free."

Next we visited the presidential memorials. We recognized the Lincoln Memorial right away. It's the one on the back of a penny. A 19-foot-tall statue of President Lincoln met us at the top of the stairs. We read his words from the Gettysburg Address **engraved**

The Wall at the Vietnam Veterans Memorial is a striking reminder of the soldiers who died or went missing during the Vietnam War. The memorial is often adorned with letters or small objects left behind to honor the lost. Some of these items are on display at the Smithsonian.

in the marble and wondered if the big ideas made the statue seem even bigger.

The Franklin Delano Roosevelt, or FDR, Memorial was next on our list. This memorial is a large park, with statues and waterfalls commemorating FDR's presidency. "He led the country through the Great Depression, and through most of World War II," Mr. Porter said. He held up a nickel from his pocket to show us where we were going next. "The Jefferson Memorial was designed after the famous Pantheon in Rome." Some of Jefferson's writings were inscribed on the wall. Mr. Porter gave us each a paper copy of the Declaration of Independence. "Quick quiz," he announced. "There are several places where the text on the wall and the real Declaration in your hands don't match. Who can find them first?"

We looked across the Tidal Basin to find our last stop. The Washington Monument was named to honor the city's founder. A one-minute elevator ride took us to the top. Thanks to the gorgeous weather, we had a full, bird's-eye view of buildings and monuments we had visited throughout the week. Looking out in all directions, we could appreciate the orderly streets from L'Enfant's design, and the beautiful hills and rivers that made George Washington choose this site as the heart of our country.

Our last day in town was the Fourth of July. We got up early and saved our seats along Constitution Avenue to see the famous Independence Day parade.

From the top of the Washington Monument, Natalie could see the Lincoln Memorial and miles beyond. Visitors used to have to hike up 897 steps to get to the top. Now they must take an elevator.

The National Independence Day Parade celebrates America's birthday in style. Each year, marching bands, floats, and VIPs are specially selected to represent the country's diversity.

There were soldiers, marching bands, dancers, and floats. Mr. Porter told us that organizers try to include something to represent each of the 50 states. After the parade, we strolled around the National Mall. We listened to a reading of the Declaration of Independence at the National Archives. At dark, we sat near the Capitol Building and listened to the National Symphony Orchestra play, just before colorful fireworks shot into the air from the Washington Monument.

Fireworks over the Washington Monument

Just The Facts

Founded: July 16, 1790

Location: Maryland-Virginia border

Form of Government: Mayor and City Council

Land Area: 68.3 Square Miles

Population: 572,059 in 2000 census; 2006 estimates show a population of 581,530 in the district itself, with 5.3 million in the larger metro area

Percent of Population Under 18: 19.8%

U.S. Rank: The 21st most populous city in the U.S.

Density: Approximately 9,378 people per square mile

Highest Point: Tenleytown at 410 feet

Lowest Point: Sea Level

Average High: 66°F* (yearly)

Average Low: 48°F (yearly)

Hottest Day: July 20, 1930 & August 16, 1918, when a temperature of 106°F was recorded

Coldest Day: February 11, 1899 when a temperature of −15°F was recorded

Hottest Month: July (Average high 89°F)

Coldest Month: January (Average low 24°F)

Average Annual Precipitation: 39.3 inches of rain, 15 inches of snow

Major Industries: Government, Tourism, Research, Education, Medicine

Latitude: 38° 53'N

Longitude: 77° 2'W

Major Neighborhoods: National Mall, Capitol Hill, Georgetown, Foggy Bottom, DuPont Circle, Downtown

Public Parks: National Mall, Rock Creek Park, Theodore Roosevelt Island, Chesapeake and Ohio Canal National Historical Park, Anacostia Park

Major Sports Teams: Nationals—Baseball; Wizards—Basketball; Capitals—Hockey; Redskins—Football; DC United—Soccer

Major Museums and Cultural Centers: The Smithsonian Institution Museums, the National Archives, John F. Kennedy Center for the Performing Arts, Meridian National Center, many embassies

*All weather statistics, U.S. National Weather Service, 2007

CRAFT TIME

Make Your Own Historical Document

What You Need:

Typing paper
    (or printer paper)
Cookie sheet with sides
Cold coffee or tea
    (about ½ cup)
Paintbrush

Sink
Watch or clock
Hair dryer
Markers
String

What You Do:

1. Rip little bits from around the edges of your paper. This will make the paper look worn and fragile. If you want your parchment to look really well-worn, you can also crumple it up.

2. Flatten the paper and place it in a cookie sheet.

3. Pour some cold coffee or tea in the cookie sheet. Use a paintbrush to cover the entire sheet in coffee or tea. Soak the paper for 5 minutes.

4. Hold your soaked paper over an empty sink where it can drip. Dry it on both sides with a hair dryer.

5. Make your own messages or decrees on the parchment paper. You could even re-create some of our country's most important documents, like the Constitution, the Declaration of Independence, or the Bill of Rights. Images of the real things and their text can be found at The National Archives' online exhibit, called "Charters of Freedom" (http://www.archives.gov/exhibits/charters/charters.html). Make your message look really authentic using a writing art called calligraphy. You can practice with some examples at http://www.mmwindowtoart.com/wordart.html

6. Roll your paper up and tie it with a string.

Washington, D.C., Historical Timeline

1790 On July 9, Congress passes the Residence Act. The law sets aside land in Maryland along the Potomac River for the nation's new capital, allowing President George Washington to pick a site within that area.

1791 On January 24, George Washington chooses a site where the Potomac and Anacostia Rivers meet.

1791 Pierre L'Enfant arrives from France on March 9 to help George Washington plan the new city. A month later, Andrew Ellicott and his assistant Benjamin Banneker begin surveying the site.

1791 L'Enfant presents his plan to Washington on June 22.

1800 On November 1, the second president of the United States, John Adams, becomes the first resident of the newly built President's House.

1814 The Capitol and the White House are set on fire and partially destroyed on August 24, as attacking British forces burn most of the government buildings in D.C.

1846 On August 10, Congress creates the Smithsonian Institution, as requested by British scientist James Smithson, who bequeathed half a million dollars for the cause.

1850 On September 20, Congress makes it illegal to trade slaves in D.C.

1861 Southern forces attack Fort Sumter on April 12, starting the Civil War.

1852 Congress frees D.C. slaves on April 16.

1889 The National Zoo is founded.

1901 The Washington Senators play baseball as one of the first eight teams of the American League.

1922 On May 30, The Lincoln Memorial is dedicated.

1961 Congress ratifies the Twenty-third Amendment to the Constitution, which gives D.C. a vote in presidential elections for the first time.

1963　At the Civil Rights March on D.C., Martin Luther King Jr. gives his "I have a dream" speech at the Lincoln Memorial on August 28.

1975　On January 2, under a law passed by President Richard Nixon, control of D.C.'s local government is passed from Congress to D.C.'s voters. The federal government retains ultimate authority during emergencies.

1976　Metrorail, the D.C.–area subway system, serves its first customers.

1979　Mayor Marion Barry begins his first term in office.

1982　A Constitution for the State of New Columbia is ratified by D.C.'s voters.

1995　Marion Barry begins his fourth term in office.

2001　Terrorist attacks on September 11 strike the Pentagon near Washington, D.C., among other targets. Almost 200 people are killed.

2006　Adrian Fenty becomes mayor of D.C. Groundbreaking ceremonies are held for the Martin Luther King Jr. National Memorial.

2007　National Geographic's King Tut exhibit is displayed in the National Gallery of Art.

2008　The Pentagon Memorial is dedicated on September 11 at the site of the 2001 attack.

2009　The 97th Annual Cherry Blossom Festival is held in March.

President Nixon Bowling in the White House

Further Reading

Books

Bluestone, Carol, and Susan Irwin. *Washington, D.C. Guidebook for Kids*. Washington, D.C.: Noodle Press, 2003.

Curlee, Lynn. *Capital*. New York: Simon & Schuster, 2003.

DK Publishing. *Eyewitness Travel Guide to Washington, D.C.* Claire Folkard (editor). New York: Dorling Kindersley Publishing, Inc., 2000.

Grumbach, Elizabeth Skinner. *We're There! Washington, D.C.* East Greenwich, RI: KidQuest, LLC, 2005.

Harness, Cheryl. *Ghosts of the White House*. New York: Aladdin, 2002.

McKay, Katherine. *Around Washington, D.C. with Kids*. New York: Fodor's Travel Publications, 2000.

Internet Sources

Duke Ellington's Washington
http://www.pbs.org/ellingtonsdc

Experience D.C. Kidzone
http://www.washington.org/visiting/
experience-dc/kidzone/fast-facts

National Gallery of Art Kids Homepage
http://www.nga.gov/kids/kids.htm

The Ruby Red Slippers, National Museum of American History

National Park Service—District of Columbia
http://www.nps.gov/state/dc/

The Virtual Smithsonian
http://2k.si.edu/

Virtual Tour of the National Mall
http://dcpages.com/Tourism/

Washington, D.C. for Kids!
http://kids.dc.gov/kids_main_content.html

White House Kids' Site
http://www.whitehouse.gov/kids/

Further Reading

Works Consulted

Brown, George Rothwell. *Washington: A Not Too Serious History*. Baltimore: The Norman Publishing Co., 1930.

Bustard, Bruce I. *Washington: Behind the Monuments*. Washington, D.C.: The National Archives and Records Administration, 1990.

DC Pages.
http://www.dcpages.com/

Epstein, Sam, and Beryl Epstein. *Washington, D.C.: The Nation's Capital*. New York: Franklin Watts, 1981.

Evelyn, Douglas E., and Paul Dickson. *On This Spot: Washington, D.C.* Washington, D.C.: Farragut Publishing Company, 1992.

Lonely Planet.
http://www.lonelyplanet.com/
worldguide/usa/washington-dc/

National Geographic Traveler: Washington, D.C. Barbara A. Noe (editor). Washington, D.C.: National Geographic Society, 2008.

Antawn Jamison, Washington Wizards forward

Rubin, Beth. *Frommer's Washington, D.C. with Kids*. Hoboken, N.J.: Wiley Publishing, Inc., 2004.

Surkiewicz, Joe, and Eve Zibart. *The Unofficial Guide to Washington, D.C.* Hoboken, N.J.: John Wiley & Sons, Inc., 2005.

Thompson, John. *Washington, D.C.: A Smithsonian Book of the Nation's Capital*. Washington, D.C.: Smithsonian Institution, 1992.

Washington, D.C.
http://www.dc.gov/

PHOTO CREDITS: pp. 4, 16, 26—Barbara Marvis; p. 8—Richard Lapsley; pp. 9, 28, 36, 38—JupiterImages; pp. 10, 12, 21, 40, 41—Library of Congress; p. 13—Architect of the Capitol; p. 18—Mark Wilson/Getty Images; p. 20—Getty Images; p. 30—Smithsonian Institution; p. 37—Hisham Ibrahim/Getty Images. All other pictures—Creative Commons.

Glossary

abolish (uh-BAH-lish)—Get rid of; do away with.

ambitious (am-BIH-shus)—Wanting to reach tough goals.

anthropologist (an-throh-PAH-luh-jist)—A scientist who studies how ancient humans lived.

attractions (uh-TRAK-shuns)—Things to see.

bequeath (bee-KWEETH)—Pass on personal property or money after death.

Congressperson (KON-gres-per-son)—Someone elected to serve in the U.S. House of Representatives or the U.S. Senate.

diffusion (dih-FYOO-zhun)—Spreading out.

engrave (en-GRAYV)—Carve into metal or stone.

federal (FEH-duh-rul)—Having to do with the national government of the United States.

franchise (FRAN-chyz)—A company that is part of a larger business.

massacre (MAA-suh-kur)—The killing of many people.

podium (POH-dee-um)—A platform for speakers.

protest (PROH-test)—Disagree through words or actions, especially with the government or a business.

quarters (KWOR-ters)—Living areas.

sandblast—To scratch a surface using fast-blown sand.

surveyor (sur-VAY-ur)—A person trained to map out an area.

terrorist (TAYR-ur-ist)—Someone who uses violence or threats to influence people.

unemployment (un-em-PLOY-munt)—joblessness.

wards—Small areas or neighborhoods within a city.

Index

ABOUT THE AUTHOR

A versatile author, Claire O'Neal has written several children's books for Mitchell Lane Publishers, including *How to Convince Your Parents You Can Care for a Pet Horse* and *Extreme Snowboarding with Lindsey Jacobellis*. She holds degrees in English and Biology from Indiana University, and a Ph.D. in Chemistry from the University of Washington. She lives in Delaware, less than two hours' drive from Washington, D.C., with her husband, two young sons, and a fat black cat. In the nation's capital, her favorite places to visit are the dinosaur hall at the National Museum of Natural History and the National Mall.